Manku

Haiku From A Man's Point Of View

Manku

Haiku From A Man's Point Of View

John F. Rowles

First Edition

J4 Music & Composition, LLC

Manku
Haiku From A Man's Point Of View

J4MC

J4 Music & Composition, LLC
Herndon, VA 20170, U.S.A.
www.j4musicandcomposition.com
john@j4musicandcomposition.com

ISBN-13: 978-0-9915926-1-6
ISBN-10: 0991592611

Copyright © 2014 by John F. Rowles

Printed in the United States of America

All rights reserved. The reproduction or utilization of this work in whole or in part in any form by any electronic, mechanical, or other means, now known or hereafter invented, including xerography, photocopying, and recording, or in any information storage or retrieval system, is forbidden without the written permission of the author.

This is a work of fiction. Names, characters, places, and incidents are either the product of the author's imagination or are used fictitiously, and any resemblance to actual persons, living or dead, business establishments, events or locales is entirely coincidental.

Cover design: Kevin Richardson
Kebo Designs, LLC
http://kebodesigns.com
kebo@kebodesigns.com

Illustrations: J. Schuh
http://jschuhguru.com
texasanimator@gmail.com

Editing: Colleen Sproull

Acknowledgments

I would like to thank the following families and individuals that contributed their time, talents, support, inspiration, and encouragement to make Manku come to life:

The Rowles Family, The Schoenholtz Family, The Pace family, Dwayne and Cindy Determan, Randy and Kelly Outman, Jerry and Daun Outman, Cindy Schrader, Kevin Richardson, J. Schuh, Colleen Sproull.

To my wife Rebecca and our daughters Erica, Kadidja, and Taylor

Chapter 1
Being a Man

Being a man means
Showing up for all you can
Because you're 'sposed to

Being a man, you
Have lost every argument;
By default you're wrong

Being a man can
Bring children to your feet, 'cause
They want your money

Eyebrows as a boy
Are ignored until the day
Girls are important

Eyebrows as a man
Go in directions unknown
To any compass

Playing a sport should
Come natural 'til we try
Doing what we can't

Our favorite team
Is clutch or choke at the time
We are not watching

We complain during
All sports in all seasons, it's
Our one true duty

If racing is your
Sport of choice, then you can be
Southern for the day

Football brings out the
Vocal tendencies we wish
We had with our boss

Baseball is only
Exciting at the game, else
It's naptime at home

Golf brings frustration
Beyond normal levels of
Swearing in public

Bowling has a great
Air of accomplishment when
We roll a beer frame

Fantasy leagues mean
Just that, it's a fantasy;
No seriousness

Win or lose, for some,
Is reason enough to waste
The next day at work

Championships should
Be a grand experiment
In gluttonous fun

Championships are
Best when served cold, except for
Florida teams...HA!

Racing has a base,
Loyal fans baked in the sun;
Cheap beer rehydrates

"Is this all there is?"
Asked a man who wasn't heard
By any woman

Don't let other men
Convince you otherwise that
Bad habits don't ROCK!

There's nothing better
Than being a man throughout
The other three weeks

Thanks to our gritty
Social skills, we men are quite
Content with silence

At home: a day off,
Honey-do's after coffee;
Motivation lacks

All West teams playing
The finals on the East Coast
Is ridiculous

Vacuuming the house
Makes for a happy wife and
Earns us a sammich

Our dog Winnie is
A furry food processor
And poop-factory

Using our sleeve as
A napkin is what guys do;
Manners optional

Remembering when
Life was simple and docile;
Then we grew up...DAMN!

I think, therefore I
Cannot believe there are so
Many un-thinkers

Don't limit yourself,
Iambic pentameter
Is just a dull box

Corn chips make for a
Meal-substitute, in the place
Of what's good for you

Squirrels are natures'
Beastly menace to our deck;
Pellet gun in hand

Music is the Earth's
Universal language; so
Is paying the bills

A man is not much
Concerned with manners, because
He's wired for sports

If our favorite
Team fails to come through, then we
Take pause for swearing

Yelling at the game
Won't make the refs ears, but will
Make it up the stairs

Men, crying is fine…
It only takes one bad call
To blow the playoffs

Championship games,
Pinnacle for the best teams,
As your team sits home

Metric or standard -
Why aren't cars all built the same?
Counterproductive

Laundry hampers don't
Get enough credit; they work
Quite well as targets

Being content works,
As long as you understand
Yard work never ends

Men need sports highlights
Without them, no conversing…
Solitude instead

Bombs, explosions, boobs,
Entertainment for all men;
Uncomplicated

Pre-game presents points
Men know they can understand;
It's all we have left

Castle Queens, world rule
Cats rule all the internet;
Castle Kings rule gone

Farting in public
Allows for entertainment
For those not downwind

Mow lawn in Summer,
Rake leaves in Fall all-the-day,
Pre-game missed each time

No logic needed,
Pre- and post-game reporting
Builds statistics skills

Chapter 2
Bathroom

The purpose of a
Man's morning is to tear up
The only bathroom

Toilet seats are cold,
Buns are shocked upon contact;
Sphincter condenses

Never disturb men
On the throne, it's the time we
Need to be ourselves

King's throne can back up,
Over it we stand amazed;
Colon good and cleansed

Streaks in the toilet
Belong to poo not ready
For the drain of death

Toilets are the throne
By which Castle Kings decide
What tasks to ignore

If the commode were
Truly a throne, the king would
Be his own jester

Commodes brings magic,
Plenty of ideas conceived…
Doubtful follow through

Sounds from the commode,
Eerie yet satisfying;
Echoes bring laughter

No better feeling
Than unloading your bladder;
Relief is priceless

Throne circumference
Should be an ample target;
Aim overrated

Pubic hair scattered,
Spots not easily vacuumed;
Can stay right there

Mats for the tile floor,
Collectors of all that falls;
Pubic steel wool pads

There is no excuse
For leaving hair on the soap,
It stays forever

Shaving is the one
Tradition passed from one whipped
Husband to the next

Trimming facial hair,
Only because she said so;
There's no debating

Trimmings from your beard,
Rest assured, will clog drains when
Your wife uses it

Castle Queen's bathroom,
Where anything she decides;
Castle Kings conform

Her sink is her sink,
Your sink is not yours ever ---
Cosmetic workbench

Bathtubs are used for
A woman's relaxation…
And for scaling fish

A man's blade should not
Become a means for women
To dull with leg hair

Bathtubs have purpose,
Deep crevasses of storage;
Hunting gear fits well

Showers are for work,
Weekends are for relaxing...
Hygiene optional

Your shower caddy,
Storage for empty bottles;
None of them are yours

Fog free mirrors hang,
Collect steam and build a skin;
False advertising

Socks are projectiles,
Rolled up smelly basket balls
Fly to the hamper

The men's room at work
Shows little care for nostrils…
Please courtesy flush

Mouthwash hides bad breath,
Should not have had so much beer,
But the game was on

Man caves are just that,
Meant as estrogen free zones...
With your own bathroom

Recliner toilets
Have lots of advantages...
Sit there forever

There should be no stress,
Bathroom acts as asylum…
Until kids find you

Explain why it is,
Ventilation works poorly
When we need it most

Always warn the Queen
Before she enters the can;
Left behind funk kills

Never cross the Queen,
Replace the toilet paper...
Over not under

What you say and do
She will always remember;
Don't forget to flush

Chapter 3
Marriage

Marriage social rank,
Women contemplate one thing:
Men are always wrong

Arguing futile,
Will has been broken in two;
Estrogen prevails

Compromise, we don't;
Oblige and obey whilst you
Part with testicles

Men rule the remote!
Unwilling to compromise;
Post-game show is on

Honey-dos are tasks,
Contemplating completion;
Eagerness runs low

Actualizing
The demands of honey-dos;
Unachievable

Honey-don'ts are things
Women ask us not to do
Until they say so

The truth must be told,
She is always right not you;
She'll tell you the same

Conflict in the home,
Men are the subject of scorn;
Dishes still aren't done

"Making-up" wisdom,
Once you admit no way out…
Jewelry is a start

When she is angry
Credit card must be at hand;
Retail therapy

Queen of the castle
Won't fully appreciate
Castle King napping

Since we have been banned
From fixing appliances,
House damage no more

This question she asks,
"Do I look good in this dress?"…
Do I look stupid?

Admitting mistakes,
Men should never follow with:
"Whatever it was"

There is no shame in
Bowing to whims of fancy
When you've pissed her off

Queen wants couple-time,
Shopping is what she suggests;
Go…feign interest

Honey-do list grows,
Relaxing time becomes an
Endangered species

Castle Queen says NO!
Castle King throws a tantrum;
Desserts not allowed

Sneaking snacks leads to
Thinking on your feet when caught;
Ninja skills have failed

Bills don't stop coming,
You are charged with finances;
Math skill set challenged

Happy wives bring joy,
Under other conditions,
There is hell to pay

A wife scorned is bad,
She will find out what you've done;
She controls your guilt

No shame giving in,
Whether you like it or not,
She will get her way

'Til death do us part,
Those words are a literal
Warning to behave

No better feeling,
Showing appreciation;
Doing the dishes

She deserves the best,
Always treat her with respect;
She grants permissions

Finances are yours,
Invest in erasers; your
Math skills are at stake

Mom, wife, and daughters,
Even the dog is female…
Epic estrogen

Men just don't get it,
She says what she wants because
Either way, you're screwed

She's counting on you,
Men are committed creatures;
Go kill the spiders

Just have to say it,
Men are hunter-gatherers…
Then marriage happens

Tell her she's pretty,
Whisk her away to lands far;
Kids fend for themselves

Never say never
Unless Castle Queen says so…
Argument over

She wants a chick-flick,
You want something she doesn't…
Like you have a choice

She loves you enough
To put up with your habits,
Do the same for her

Ask for permission,
Without it you will pay big;
Tattoo brings forth hell

She takes care of you
Even though she's not your mom,
'Cause that would be weird

Chapter 4
Kids

Dads have challenges,
Pre-game or post-game or both?
Wife, kids, work, win out

New dads are challenged,
Poopy diapers smell rotten;
Nausea ensues

Seasoned dads ponder,
New dads are full of unknown;
Diaper still not changed

Kids and dads the same,
Love to play and love to laugh,
Love to avoid mom

Children do grow up,
Dads have done all they can do;
They'll call for money

When kids need a talk,
Dads are stern with their voices…
Until mom steps in

Daughters are a joy!
Daddy's little girls will school
You with their logic

You chase off suitors,
She chides you with disdain and
Thanks you for caring

Daughters are to dads
Life's greatest joy, equal that
To post-game highlights

Though I raise my voice,
The wrongdoing committed;
Grounded you will be

Make what's important
For her as important to
You and win her heart

Playing in the mud,
Teaching kids laughter; and the
Fun will never end

Dads do what they can
And daughters do what they want;
Both one and the same

Never judge a child,
Encouragement; their mistakes
Will turn to wisdom

Wagging your finger,
Kids are captivated by
The wag RPM

Pride in your children
Shows through your reassurance;
They will be ok

Stepchildren may not
Be yours, love them like they are,
Treat them as your own

Trusting a young child
With paying attention is
Unwise, says mommy

Are you watching her?
Or are you keeping an eye?
Mommy says do both

Potty training is,
Infuriating so much…
Bribing sometimes works

Is it possible
Children have magical reach?
Cookies are now gone

Please don't tell mommy
You caught us eating corn chips;
Diet will result

Dating my daughter,
You will not disrespect her,
Else earn a pounding

Watering the lawn
Produces so much mischief,
Run through the sprinkler

Driving you will not!
My car is valuable…
Take mom's car instead

Meaning at 16:
Getting a job would be…wait,
What was I thinking?

Applying makeup,
Dad's face is a clean canvas;
She'll make you pretty

Applying makeup,
For a date later tonight;
She's grown up too fast

Discipline is key,
They're not listening; but hope
You got through to them

A child's homework done,
Last minute checks reveal it
Was due three days past

Money you can have,
Where has yours disappeared, wait…
Clean room, mow yard…Earn

Your room is a sty!
I did not raise any pigs!
Barnyard this is not!

Where is the remote?
Undiscovered dimension?
Interrogate kids

Is there any child
Immune from pulling fingers?
Guffaws will follow!

Smart phones have become
A sign of the beast; constant
Zombies on display

Grandchildren appear,
Hugs, tickle, candy, soda;
And then give them back

Chapter 5
Work

Work should be a place
Where careers blossom, instead…
Same shit tomorrow

At work gossip kills,
Your favorite team still sucks;
Expect ridicule

Cubicle fodder,
Kid pics, trolls, toys, distractions;
Work secondary

Deadlines loom over,
Great pressure to deliver
While execs play golf

Cube-farms aplenty,
No doors or windows, all are
Tiny work-free zones

Bosses above us,
Promotion still perplexing;
Brown-nosing expert

IT industry,
Full of bright young minds not yet
Jaded by real world

Develop programs,
Written to requirements;
Miracles assumed

Mainframe or server,
Customer never happy;
They think it's magic

Repeated meetings,
Conference calls never end;
Endless blathering

Conference calls prove
All on the call are experts;
None are proficient

Cubicle manners,
Workmates fart and pick their nose;
Etiquette lacking

Taking ownership:
Being accountable for
Traversing bullshit

What is worse than more
Team building exercises?
I hate these people!

Office politics
Stymie ideas to languish
In circular files

Resume touted
Degree, certification…
Yet still a dumbass

You expect me to
Pull a rabbit out of my
Ass…take a number

Submit a ticket,
We will promptly see to it
When we give a shit

At some point, IT
Will finally get it right;
Contractors cheaper

Tinderbox desktop:
Piled papers, safety hazard,
Fodder for bonfire

Too much strong cologne!
No need to bathe in it; please
Stop burning nostrils

Relative progress
Meets the set deadline until
Poor planning exposed

Break room gossiping:
Solving corporate issues
Ignored by bosses

Don't send an email
Without re-reading it first...
Send button is cursed

Structure in IT
Helps build customer service
Until C-suite whim

Without our workmates
Projects fall to the wayside;
We blame the PMs

Annual picnics,
We all seem to agree that
Veggie burgers suck

Annual reviews,
Management tells us we're great;
Raises speak softly

Office supply thief,
Ninja of the stolen pen;
Gone are the staplers

Atmosphere is key,
Production improves only
If management out

Our scrutinized past
Haunts us for work clearances;
Spring break was worth it

Working with shitheads
Can be infuriating,
Their thoughts are toilets

Working with people
With gnat-like attention spans
Is worse than daycare

"Ad hoc" is a queue
Where people's bad ideas go
Wait for feigned interest

Cubicles at work,
Are small jails for prairie dogs
And not for humans

Disillusionment
Happens between 12 and 2;
Lunch coma time frame

Popcorn at work makes
The entire floor jump up
To see who to blame

Chapter 6
General

When trying new food
Don't trust anyone who says
"This is delicious"

Man-pets of all kinds:
Dogs, cats, fish, ferrets, badgers…
Yes, I said badgers

If your dog eats poo,
Encourage it to lick on
Everyone else first

DIY projects
Make you look manly until
Reading instructions

Cats have their own style,
Attention at their leisure;
A four-legged man

Romance your wife with
Dinner, dancing, chick-flick; then
Beg to watch highlights

False advertising,
"Wrinkle free" shirts just not true;
Ironing futile

Laundry isn't done,
Wife won't touch your nasty stuff;
Learn to wipe better

Men care not about
Furniture shopping unless
Local game blackout

Mortgage and a job,
All the hell one man can stand;
Playoffs bring respite

Shoveling driveway,
Snow has ruined another
Afternoon of sports

Traffic is a pain,
Construction work is behind;
Blame politicians

Christmas lights in June,
Neighbor is smart or lazy...
Clever either way

Going to the gym,
Probably get serious
At some point in time

24-hour news
Has made the world much smaller;
Informed woebegone

Vacation money,
Better spent on student loans;
Cruiselines lack hygiene

Public restrooms are
A place where people decide
Against etiquette

Politics purchased,
Worst investment the public
Never elected

Politicians shame,
Soulless elected people;
Full of excuses

House decoration,
Never for the lighthearted;
Not at all for men

Basic cable cheap,
Network television sucks,
Sports is our escape

What is a chaise lounge?
Confusing couch with one arm...
Who designs this stuff?

Men don't care what's on,
We care for what else is on;
Kings of the remote!

The impossible
Made possible through wholesale;
Big boxes of crap

Pick up the dog poo,
It ricochets while mowing;
Deadly brown missiles

Grocery shopping,
Aisle after aisle after aisle…
Can't find the chip dip

Chapter 7
Growing Old

Gray hair is sudden,
Some are earned, some genetic,
All signify age

Why hair in the ears?
Is this a cruel joke or is
It evolution?

The waistband spare tire
Should not be the same girth as
The one in the trunk

We are obsolete...
Children work gadgets designed
For much younger eyes

Retire and relax,
Earned the right to bitch about
Government full time

Elastic crucial,
Allows for the round middle
To fit into pants

Gray hair has no shape,
In all directions it flies;
Why bother combing?

Men in youth play hard,
With age the body wears out;
Chiropractor saves

Annual checkup:
Violated every year
By a plastic glove

Looking back, a man
Sees transgressions in the hope
That more are coming

"Turn your head and cough"...
When the doctor is cupping,
These words bring no joy

Colonoscopy,
Prep brings out the worst in you,
Toilet will curse you

Screenings are a must,
No excuse for avoidance,
Co-pay is worth it

Cheese doesn't sit well,
Colon blocked with dairy slab…
Beer may push it out

A man's head goes bald,
Hair follicles start to die;
Nature's little fib

Immobility:
The realization you
Can't reach the remote

Short, tall, skinny, fat
Four stages of life for men;
Progress in between

Aging is no curse,
Immaturity won't wane;
Helps us to stay young

Memory goes first,
Past you may not remember,
Others will recall

The second is sight,
Glasses or contacts for life
Keep getting thicker

The third is hearing,
Tuning out bullshit is great...
Life just got better

Performance is last,
Now it's just a good night's sleep;
Life just got boring

"You get off my lawn!"
Words that show a tell tale sign
You are now your dad

Chapter 8
The End

The final Manku,
Hopefully these provoked thought
And a few laughs too

www.ingramcontent.com/pod-product-compliance
Lightning Source LLC
Chambersburg PA
CBHW071259040426
42444CB00009B/1787